GRIEVANCE AND DISCIPLINE IN SCHOOLS

Other titles in this series

Effective Staff Selection in Schools, by Colin Hume

Also from Longman

Effective Local Management of Schools, edited by Brian Fidler and G
    Bowles

Managing the National Curriculum, edited by Tim Brighouse and
    Bob Moon

Managing School Time, by Brian Knight

Staff Appraisal in Schools and Colleges, edited by Brian Fidler and
    Robert Cooper

GRIEVANCE AND DISCIPLINE IN SCHOOLS

Colin Hume

Longman

Published by Longman Industry and Public Service Management, Longman Group UK Limited, 6th Floor, Westgate House, The High, Harlow, Essex CM20 1YR, England and Associated Companies throughout the world.
Telephone: Harlow (0279) 442601
Fax: Harlow (0279) 444501
Telex: 81491 Padlog

British Library Cataloguing in Publication Data
Hume, Colin
    Grievance and discipline in schools — (Longman/AGIT school governor training series).
    1. Great Britain. Schools. Teachers. Discipline
    I. Title
    371.1′00941

    ISBN 0–582–06255–1

ISBN 0-582-06255-1

1164 7 104566 120

Phototypeset by Input Typesetting Ltd, London

Printed by Bell and Bain Ltd., Glasgow

Contents

Chapter 1

Introduction

Key points

- Substantial change in the role of governors
- Grievance and discipline become school-based
- All governors must be prepared to be involved in grievance and discipline
- Correct handling of grievance and discipline is a contribution towards effective staff management

Local Management of Schools (LMS) started to come into operation in England and Wales from April 1990. LMS means a substantial change in the role of governors at school level. They are now responsible for controlling all of the school's resources. In the early days of its development LMS was seen as being mainly about the local management of financial resources. This is reflected in its previous name, Local Financial Management. The change in name recognises that staff, also, are as vital a part of the school's resources as finance. There are several important aspects to effective management of the staff resource. One is recruitment, which is covered in a companion volume. Another is grievance and discipline. This book focuses on how governors should deal with grievance and discipline under LMS.

Both grievance and discipline procedures are aimed at remedying the problems they deal with. Grievance arises when a member of staff feels dissatisfied with working conditions or considers that he or she has been a victim of harsh or unfair treatment. The grievance procedure ideally should result in an improvement in the situation. Similarly with the disciplinary procedure although it is initiated by management when a member of staff is causing concern in terms of work conduct and it is possible that the end result may be dismissal. Neither the grievance or discipline procedures should be conceived as negative activities or approached fatalistically, since in many cases the outcome will be a well-supported improvement which will be of benefit both to the member of staff concerned and the school.

Governors' responsibilities for grievance and discipline under LMS are spelt out in detail in the Education Reform Act (ERA) 1988. The Act states that 'discipline in relation to staff' and 'the procedures for the redress of grievances shall be under the control of the governing body'. It further states that the governing body 'shall establish . . . disciplinary rules and procedures and (grievance) procedures . . . ' (see para. 6 of Schedule 3 of the Education Reform Act 1988).

The involvement of school governors in staff grievance and discipline is not entirely new. In voluntary-aided schools, the governors have always been the employer and had a staff management role to some extent. In all other schools before LMS governors were involved in staff grievance and discipline but only to a limited degree. All governors of schools where LMS is in operation are responsible for controlling grievance and discipline.

Under LMS grievance and discipline becomes school-based. Any pre-LMS arrangements will need revision to take account of this. Such revision needs careful consideration, as there are a number of areas of discipline in particular where the Education Act 1988 lays down certain provisions which must be incorporated. For example, governors have the power to dismiss a member of staff but arrangements must be made for an appeal against the governors' decision. There is clearly more to revising the grievance and disciplinary procedures than a cosmetic adjustment to existing procedures. In the new school-based procedures the most important thing is that the role of school management and the governors in grievance and discipline is clear and understood by both sides from the outset.

To summarise, controlling grievance and discipline at school level will in practice involve three different aspects. The first is that the governors will be responsible for overseeing grievance and discipline. The second is that the governors will be responsible for the actual arrangements for grievance and discipline. The third is that governors can expect to be, and should be prepared to be, involved directly in grievance and discipline. This places governors at the forefront of staff management at school level. Their role will be carried out in partnership with the headteacher and senior staff of the school. Nevertheless, good staff management will hinge on the contribution made by the governing body. The ability to deal with grievance and discipline correctly will be a major part of that contribution.

There are good reasons for dealing with grievance and discipline together. In practice, there are many similarities in the way each should and must be dealt with. The number of cases arising from disciplinary procedures greatly exceeds the number arising from grievance procedures, certainly in terms of appearances before industrial tribunals. This pattern is likely to continue. Nevertheless, it would be an error to view grievance as a sort of junior partner to discipline, needing lesser treatment. As we shall see, there are some key staffing issues which can arise under grievance.

By their nature, grievance or disciplinary situations arise randomly. It may be by no means certain exactly when and at what stage governors will be involved. Usually, given little or no warning there will also be a limited time to prepare. However, some advice and support will be available from the local education authorities to help governing bodies deal with grievance and discipline.

The growth of the governors' role under LMS has implications that go beyond the education field. Governing bodies will be acting not only within education law but also within employment law. This puts school governors in a unique position in two main respects.

Firstly, grievance and discipline outside of education is normally dealt with solely by full-time managers. Even these people may find grievance and discipline situations far from easy to handle. Governors themselves may have had previous work experience in dealing with grievance and discipline. Such governors will be an asset, if they are available. However, it would be unrealistic for any governing body to attempt to rely on such individuals to deal with these issues. In practice, any and all governors should be prepared to deal with grievance and discipline if the need arises.

Secondly, industrial law expects the employer to be responsible for grievance and discipline. The employer is defined as the holder or controller of the contract of employment. As already mentioned, in voluntary-aided schools the governors are the employers. In all other schools the contract of employment for school staff is held by the Local Education Authority (LEA). There will be no change in this under LMS. However, despite not holding the contract, the governing body's duties and powers will be those of an employer in all but name.

To duties and powers can be added liabilities. Situations could arise under LMS where governing bodies find themselves called before an industrial tribunal over decisions they have made. The chances of this happening are greatly reduced if grievance and discipline is handled properly in the first place.

Effective handling of grievance and discipline requires an appreciation of what exactly is involved, what the procedures are, and how to work them. It is an area in which many governors may be wary of becoming involved. A degree of caution is justified. It is important to realise that grievance and discipline handling has a purpose. That purpose is effective staff management. If governors deal with grievance and discipline from an informed basis there is every chance that this aim can be achieved.

The approach adopted in this book is to treat grievance and discipline as separate subjects. If you only want to know about grievance, for example, reading the chapters on grievance will be sufficient. Alternatively, you can just read the section on discipline. It is not necessary to read the whole book if you are only immediately interested in one of these subjects. There is some overlap and repetition to allow for this, which bears out that similar, basic principles are involved in both grievance and discipline. Also, these basic principles can be applied to situations outside of the staff management field such as disciplinary situations involving pupils.

Chapter 2

What is grievance?

Key points

- Redress of grievances is an important right
- Grievance is a demand for corrective action
- Grievance procedures must be changed to work under LMS
- Conciliation is a necessary part of grievance handling

The right to 'redress of grievances', as the Education Reform Act describes it, is an important right for employees both individually and collectively. It is undoubtedly an ancient right recognised long before current employment law. It is now a legal right as all employers must, by law, inform their employees of the grievance arrangements in the contract of employment. The right to express a grievance is a safeguard against abuse of managerial authority. It can also be a means of ensuring a minimum standard of managerial treatment of staff.

Grievance is a demand for corrective action

In employment terms, a grievance means more than a complaint, a difference, or a statement of discontent. It means using a set-down procedure as a means for communicating the complaint, or difference or discontent to management. Moreover, it means making a demand for corrective action to be taken by management.

It is important to recognise that with grievance the member of staff is 'in the driving seat'. It is up to the member of staff pursuing the grievance to decide whether or not management's response is acceptable. Management's position is one of reacting to what is being put before them. There may or may not be a basis for the grievance. Nevertheless the responsibility of management is to respond to the grievance. That response must be made within any time limit that the procedure lays down.

Managers are only human, and some may feel that the raising of a grievance is a threat or a challenge to their authority. It can also be very frustrating if management feel that they have responded adequately but the member of staff insists on pursuing the grievance further. Any feelings of this kind need to be firmly put aside. If they are allowed to influence management's response, they will, at best, only hamper the effective operation of the grievance procedure. At worst it may result in a reluctance by other staff to use the procedure in future even if their grievances are genuine.

Under LMS, grievance means governors taking on what used to be the role of the LEA. That role included controlling the arrangements for grievance and accepting legal liability for the operation of the arrangements.

Changes required in procedure

Part of the responsibility for the arrangements is setting out a grievance procedure. There will be pre-LMS procedures which must be revised to reflect the changed position of the governing body. Some advice and assistance in changing the grievance procedure should be available from the LEA. There are variations in practice, but in some schools there may actually be separate procedures for different types of staff. It is sensible to combine these into one new grievance procedure if possible.

Any changes in the pre-LMS procedures will need to be discussed with the staff of the school. Governors will be aware that schools work in a highly unionised environment. Any such changes will also need to be the subject of formal consultations with the trade unions represented in the school.

Coming to the issue of legal responsibility, under LMS any legal action over grievance will be directed at the governing body and not the LEA. Such an action will normally be pursued through an industrial tribunal. Without dismissing it entirely, it is important to get the risk of legal action into proportion. The scope for such action over grievance is more limited than it is with discipline. Any such risk is minimised if the grievance is handled properly in the first place. The LEA will indemnify the governing body against any legal action arising from LMS. Such indemnification is still likely to require the governors to have acted in good faith and not to have breached procedures, and if they act contrary to the LEA's advice they will be required to meet the costs from the school budget.

The actual action that a member of staff could take if they consider they have a substantial enough grievance is to resign and then claim 'constructive dismissal'. By this they mean that the relationship between them and the school has been so damaged by the actions of management as to amount effectively to dismissal. Constructive dismissal can be hard to prove, and it is a drastic step — the member of staff has to resign first to claim it. Nevertheless if grievances are not correctly handled the possibility of constructive dismissal being upheld at a tribunal could arise.

The relatively low volume of grievances has already been mentioned. This may indicate a low level of discontent by staff generally. It may also reflect the reluctance of many members of staff to use the grievance procedure even if they have genuine grievances. No matter what the potential volume of grievances may be, governors should do everything they can to ensure that the grievance system in their school works properly. There are two ways of doing this.

First, every support should be given to staff to use the grievance procedure if they feel the need. It can be helpful to include a statement of intent in the grievance procedure. This should state management's view that any member of staff should feel free to use the procedure without fear of recrimination or future victimisation.

Secondly, if the grievance procedure is activated it must work, both for the member of staff and management. School governors must be able to make an effective contribution if they become directly involved. Staff who are trade union members are very likely to be assisted with their grievance by a trade union representative or official. This will be an additional pressure to make sure that grievance is handled properly. Flawed handling of a grievance, if it occurs, may not make the position irredeemable but it will mean the whole process becoming much longer. It may make the grievance far more difficult to resolve. The process of conciliation is likely to suffer.

The need for conciliation

The need for conciliation is an important part of any grievance procedure. If a genuine grievance is raised, a grievance procedure must do more than allow management to take corrective action. Rectifying a grievance by itself will not necessarily restore the relationship between the member of staff and their management and/or school. If the relationship has not been destroyed by the need to use the grievance procedure it will certainly have been damaged. A process of conciliation is required to restore the relationship. In other words the procedure should be constructive in intent.

In practice, appreciating exactly what a grievance procedure is, what it involves and how it operates is central to dealing with grievance effectively. How a grievance procedure might work under LMS is looked at in detail in the next chapter.

Chapter 3

Grievance procedures

Key points

- Procedures mean fairness and consistency
- What a typical grievance procedure should look like
- The rules of natural justice
- What a grievance procedure needs to cover

A procedure is not a form of bureaucratic rules or a constraint on action. A properly designed and operated grievance procedure can be an aid to effective staff management. No one would claim that grievance procedures in themselves will always lead to correct decisions but what they will do is ensure that whatever decisions are made are reached on a fair and consistent basis.

Under LMS, the direct involvement of governors in the grievance procedure will only come at the very end of the process. At the same time, the role played by the governors is a vital one. To fulfil that role an appreciation of what is involved in the whole of the grievance procedure is needed.

The basic concepts

It may be helpful to look first at the basic concepts. There are two basic concepts behind all grievance procedures.

The first concept is that of a 'staged' response to grievance. What this means is that the grievance procedure is a series of steps. Each step through the procedure draws in increasingly senior levels of school management. The final step is the governing body.

There are several reasons for this. In part, it is a recognition of how a grievance develops. If a member of staff has a grievance it may be settled purely informally as part of the day-to-day dialogue between staff and management. This may include counselling by management if they consider it appropriate.

At this point, the approach adopted is to try and resolve the grievance at the point at which it started. The first step of the procedure should involve the member of staff and their immediate manager. Only if the member of staff considers that the grievance is not resolved is a further step taken. This carries on to the end of the procedure.

This approach prevents, for example, any attempt to refer a grievance to the governors before it has been progressed through the earlier levels of the grievance procedure. The reason for not allowing this is not just bureaucratic. It is a recognition of the need and right of the school managers to manage grievance. It is also a recognition of the need for staff/management relationships to be restored. This last process in particular can become more difficult the further the procedure progresses.

A typical grievance procedure under LMS

Let us now look at a typical school grievance procedure under LMS. In describing it as typical, it should be said that there are variations in practice. The procedure can be shown diagrammatically as steps on a ladder with the level of seriousness and the level of management involved increasing as each step is taken.

Diagram 1:   Steps on the grievance procedure ladder

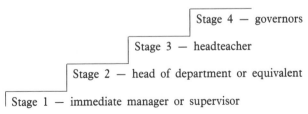

Stage 4 — governors

Stage 3 — headteacher

Stage 2 — head of department or equivalent

Stage 1 — immediate manager or supervisor

The different stages of the procedure will be considered first, and then some other essential aspects which governors need to consider.

Stage 1

'A member of staff who is aggrieved on any matter should discuss it in the first instance with his/her immediate manager or supervisor. The immediate manager or supervisor will give an oral response to the grievance as soon as possible. The response will be given within five working days.'

This bears out the aim of attempting to resolve the grievance as locally and informally as possible in the first instance. Also although time to respond to a grievance must be allowed, there must be no excessive delay. The procedure caters for both points by specifying a time limit for a response. Failure to respond within the set time limit would justify going on to the next stage regardless.

Stage 2

'If the member of staff is not satisfied with a response received under Stage 1 or if no response is received within five working days, he/she may then raise the grievance with the head of department or equivalent. The head of department or equivalent will respond as soon as possible. The response will be given within seven working days.'

This allows the next level of management to deal with the grievance maintaining the same principles featured as Stage 1.

Stage 3

'If the member of staff is not satisfied with a response received under Stage 2 or if no response is received within seven working days, he/she may then raise the grievance in writing with the headteacher. The headteacher will invite the member of staff, accompanied by a "friend" if they wish, and appropriate members of management to a meeting to discuss the grievance. The headteacher will respond to the member of staff in writing as soon as possible after the meeting. The response will be given within ten working days.' (Note: 'friend' in practice may be a trade union representative, solicitor, colleague or personal friend.)

This stage represents the last stage within the management of the school. It allows the management of the school a final opportunity to resolve the grievance before referral to the governors may occur.

Stage 4

'If the member of staff is not satisfied with a response received under Stage 3 or if no response is received within ten working days, he/she may appeal to the governing body of the school. Such an appeal should be addressed in writing to the headteacher who will ensure that the chairman of governors and the clerk to the governors are informed. The governing body will convene a grievance appeal panel. The grievance appeal panel will normally consist of the chairman of governors, and two other governors selected by the governing body. The grievance appeal panel will be convened within fifteen working days of the grievance being received. The member of staff will have the right to attend and to be accompanied by a "friend".'

This is the final stage of the procedure. As such it is the one at which the governing body should be involved. In this procedure, a panel of governors is drawn from the governing body to deal with the grievance. The basis on which this panel should work forms the second important concept behind grievance procedures. That concept is natural justice.

What is natural justice?

Law springs from two sources. One source is Acts of Parliament, the other is common law. Common law essentially derives from the cumulative decisions of courts over the years, and some of these decisions have established a framework for fair and consistent treatment of individuals in certain circumstances. This framework is known as natural justice. The source of natural justice is important, clearly any breach of natural justice is open to a successful legal challenge in a court.

To ensure that natural justice is not breached, a number of requirements need to be rigorously and carefully applied. This is particularly important where a hearing is being held, such as the one illustrated as the last stage of a formal grievance procedure.

The provisions for natural justice do not deal with the merits of a decision but how that decision is made. They are more than a statement of what fair procedure requires. They are a guarantee of the basic rights for both sides. Failure to follow the rules of natural justice is in itself grounds to challenge a decision, however fair it might otherwise be.

It may be helpful to summarise the rules of natural justice and comment on them.

1. There must be time to prepare.
    If a panel is convened, as much advance warning as possible must be given to the member of staff concerned.

2. The case must be stated and evidence produced.
    The panel must reach its decision on the basis of the evidence before it. This seems self-evident but in practice it means not allowing assumptions, prejudices or stereotypes to influence its decision.

3. There is a right of reply.
    This applies to both sides, and to any point raised in the hearing.

4. The member of staff has the right to be represented or accompanied.
    An important individual right, for that reason invariably written into the grievance procedure. There is no restriction on whom the member of staff chooses to accompany them. It is normally a trade union representative or official but it might be a solicitor, a friend or another member of staff.

5. Both sides can call and/or question witnesses.
    This is an extension of the need of the panel to make decisions on the basis of evidence. Such evidence may only be available from, or may only be supported by, witnesses. There can be no restriction on witnesses. There must be a right to cross-examination by both sides.

6. There is a right of appeal.
    A school-based grievance procedure which had as its last stage a reference to the headteacher would not accord with natural justice. It is in the interests of natural justice that a final stage allowing an appeal to the governors must be included in the procedure.

What else does a grievance procedure need to cover?

The procedure as outlined above is very basic. For such a procedure to be workable in practice, there are several issues which need to be addressed.

One is what is not covered by the grievance procedure. It should not cover anything to do with salary, payment or grading. This should be explained in a statement at the beginning of the procedure. Separate arrangements to deal with these topics are set out in the conditions of service for staff.

Another issue is the member of staff's right to be represented. In the procedure looked at, this is only allowed for at the third and final stages. Some grievance procedures allow representation at all stages. Such representation will generally be by a trade union. There may be trade union pressure for an unrestricted right of representation. Certainly in the procedure outlined, such representation could extend to Stage 2 but its extension to Stage 1 might be debatable.

There is an issue of the extent to which the governing body can delegate its responsibility for grievance. The procedure outlined provides for an appeals panel to be drawn from the governing body. In practice, no governing body could or should attempt to deal with grievance without delegation to a smaller group. The exact basis for setting up such groups is covered within the governing body regulations.

The last issue to be examined in this chapter is grievance arising from alleged discrimination on grounds of disability, race or sex. Such discrimination cannot be adequately handled by applying the grievance procedure in a straightforward manner. For example, a complaint of discrimination may well be against the manager or supervisor to whom the grievance would normally be taken.

Discrimination is an extremely serious matter. If grievances of this nature are inadequately handled it may lead to legal action against the governing body in an industrial tribunal. It is in everybody's interests that proper provision is made for dealing with this kind of grievance.

Direct and immediate reference of such grievances to the headteacher should be written into the procedure.

Chapter 4

Effective grievance handling

Key points

- Counselling — what it is and its benefits
- Governors' involvement in grievance handling
- Traps for governors
- Implications for grievance hearings
- Collective grievances

Effective grievance handling means a fine balance between the needs and rights of the individual on the one hand, and the legitimate claims and demands of the school on the other. The first part of handling grievance effectively is to consider what can be done to avoid grievances being lodged in the first place.

In any employment situation, there is always the prospect of grievances arising from the day-to-day management of the organisation. A particular decision or event may be the trigger, or a grievance may arise from what, from the member of staff's point of view, has been a long and deteriorating situation. That the grievance procedure is there to deal with the situation is not the whole answer. There is likely to be an initial reluctance by a member of staff to use it, and what is needed is a preliminary to the disciplinary procedure which offers some prospect of a solution. A potential answer to this need is counselling.

What is counselling?

Counselling of different types and in differing situations has become a trend in society generally. It is a recognition of the greater stresses in society today and a reflection of the benefits of counselling. In this instance counselling is essentially an exploratory process. Management and staff need to look at a situation together, consider the options and discuss what can and what cannot be done in a confidential and undisturbed setting.

In the context of grievance, it gives management an opportunity to be aware that a potential grievance exists and to correct it before reference to the grievance procedure is made. This should not be seen as its sole purpose. Counselling is important in its own right as well as a preliminary to a grievance being lodged.

Some managers might well query the need for counselling at all on the assumption that day-to-day contact between management and staff is enough. There are two answers. The first is that, in practice, normal staff/management contact does not provide either the opportunity or the right environment for sensitive issues to be discussed. This is particularly true when both management and staff are coping with increased workloads and pressures; those working in education today are very much in this position. It is those additional pressures which make a counselling scheme both a necessity and a vital asset.

The second answer is that counselling needs to be managed. Loosely arranged counselling schemes between management and staff are unlikely to work. The objectives of counselling, how it will work, and what it is for must be set out and made known to members of staff and management. The central issue is ensuring that confidentiality will be maintained. Some employers have schemes which involve management keeping a record of counselling on a member of staff's personal file. There must be considerable doubts about whether most members of staff would use such a scheme, and most are likely to prefer that no record is kept. If a scheme is operated where a record is kept, in most instances this is only with the specific agreement of the member of staff concerned who has the right to both see the proposed record, sign it and comment on it if he or she wishes. Also any such records lapse after a specified period has elapsed, e.g. after a year.

Introducing a counselling scheme is not likely to be entirely straightforward. A degree of concern may be aroused among staff. Trade unions are likely to be suspicious. Certainly the introduction of counselling will need consultation with both staff and trade unions. Again, the key issue is likely to be confidentiality. This can only be achieved in practice through a carefully managed scheme where management is fully aware of what the scheme is for and what management's role is.

As part of their responsibility for making arrangements for grievance and discipline, governors have every right to ask for proposals for a counselling scheme to be drawn up. This can and should involve advice from the LEA. There are limits to what will be possible in schools under LMS. Some organisations, for example, employ counsellors or hire outside counsellors or counselling organisations. This will just not be possible in schools. Counselling will, therefore, be an addition to existing managerial responsibilities. The drawback remains that staff may be reluctant to take problems to existing managers within the school, in case it acts to their detriment. Although the context of the study was a large organisation, and it was therefore possible to use staff who did not know those they were counselling, there is some evidence that counselling schemes operated by internal management do work, that stress levels are reduced and staff work better. (See, for example, 'A Post Office Initiative to Stamp out Stress' — *Personnel Management*, August 1989.) A properly managed counselling scheme can be a positive aid to effective staff management.

Governor involvement in grievance handling

Even with a counselling scheme and the fact that, in practice, grievance procedures will be seen by staff as a 'last resort', members of staff may consider they have no option but to use the grievance procedure.

The second part of grievance handling for governors is actual involvement, essentially at the end of the process, as an appeal committee. This means that all stages of the procedure up to that level fall to the headteacher and other management staff of the school. It follows that the governors should not expect detailed reports from the headteacher on grievance within the lower levels of the procedure. Nor, in order to preserve their appeal committee role, should governors be tempted to open up discussion of such cases at governors' meetings.

All governors need to be prepared to be involved in grievance hearings. It may be rare for a member of staff to pursue a grievance this far, but if it happens there can be no guarantee as to which governors will be available to form the panel. The chair or vice-chair of governors should certainly be designated to chair any meeting of the panel. A clerk is necessary to both set up the meeting and keep a basic record of what happened. This can be the clerk of governors provided that they are not involved in the presentation of the case before the panel in any way.

Although they may opt not to be involved, governors who are also members of staff at the school are not debarred from sitting on grievance panels.

The most important thing about a grievance hearing is that all the parties will be working within the rules of natural justice. A definition of natural justice has been given in the previous chapter. For a grievance hearing to work requires more than a fair and consistent approach.

One major issue that arises is what the role of the governors should be. Some governors may well assume that it is essentially a passive one, restricted to judging the case on the information presented to them. On the contrary, governors should participate fully and question and cross-question both sides and any witnesses in order to clarify points.

Doing this requires essentially the same skills as are used during selection interviews. The key words are 'who', 'what', 'when', 'why' and 'how' — in other words, open questions. Closed or 'yes/no' questions should be avoided. Another important technique is funnelling, a series of open questions followed by a closed one narrowing down on a particular point. For example, 'how did you find out?', 'when did you find out?' followed by, 'wouldn't you agree you were wrong not to check the facts with the head of department?'

Traps for governors

It is important that governors take notes during the grievance hearing and that these notes are kept, since there is the possibility that subsequent referral to an industrial tribunal could occur. These notes should include an outline of questions asked and answers received.

Grievance hearings do pose some potential traps for governors. Examples of points to watch for are:

1. Only ask questions that are relevant to the case before you. Avoid leading questions, that is, a question prompting a particular answer.

2. Do not allow assumptions, prejudices or stereotypes to influence your decision. The approach should be an evidential one, i.e. what decision does the weight of evidence support?

3. You are entitled to assess the credibility of witnesses and the extent to which you accept or reject some or all of their evidence.

4. The value of hearsay evidence can be questionable but it should not be excluded as part of a case.

The most important thing for the panel is to correctly identify all the facts of the case. It is then necessary to judge whether what is claimed is correct or whether a misunderstanding has arisen. The purpose of the hearing is to solve the grievance if possible. Subject to an assessment of exactly what has happened, it is then a question of developing a solution.

The factors which the panel need to consider are what the constraints are, and what common ground there is. The governors should not see their decision to be one of either conceding or rejecting the grievance in its entirety. Nor should governors see their role as one of backing the school management regardless of the circumstances. The approach should be one of attempting to develop a solution based on an evaluation of the facts. This will involve an evaluation of what the constraints are, what the possibilities are, and what common ground, if any, exists.

Some idea of what could be involved is given in the three grievance case studies which appear in Chapter 9.

Implications of grievance hearings

The priority in a grievance hearing is to solve the individual case before the panel. It is important that the panel should see its role as purely that. If a grievance is upheld, the implications for the school need to be identified. The governing body as a whole needs to be involved in this.

This raises the question of to what extent the details of any grievance hearing should be reported to the governing body as a whole. Clearly no report at all would be unsatisfactory but at the same time some care is needed depending on the circumstances of the individual case. As a general rule, it is not relevant or necessary to identify members of staff by name during any report to the governing body. Grievances may be upheld which have been caused by failings of individual members of the management team. In most cases this will not raise the issue of disciplinary action but it may do so if for example discrimination has been found on grounds of disability, race or sex.

The best advice is that no report should be made on a grievance hearing until the issue of possible disciplinary action has been dealt with. A discussion of such a case could compromise the governing body's role as a disciplinary appeal committee. It would be reasonable in this situation for the chair of governors to report that a grievance panel has upheld a grievance but in view of possible disciplinary action no detailed report could be made to the governing body for the present time.

The purpose of any report to the governing body is to identify whether a grievance has arisen because of some failing in the school's staff management policies, procedures and practices. If that is the case, then the governing body must ask for prompt corrective action to be taken.

Collective grievances

No discussion of grievance handling can be complete without mentioning the issue of collective grievances. These may arise particularly under LMS in relation to a decision by the school management or governors or both. It may also arise from circumstances that existed prior to LMS and which may not be of the current school management's or governors' making. A collective grievance is simply a grievance affecting a group of staff and pursued by them as a group. Sometimes a whole series of individual grievances may be raised all around the same issue, and in practice this would be deemed to be a collective grievance.

In handling collective grievances, the focus is clearly not on the individuals concerned and the grievance hearing as such is more likely to be a three-way meeting-point between governors, management and trade union representatives. Otherwise collective grievances should be handled within the same framework of natural justice as other grievances. The exception is that the governing body needs to decide whether it wishes to delegate a decision to the normal grievance panel. Some governors may press for the whole governing body to be involved. This needs to be considered carefully. One problem of course would be appeals, some sort of external body would be required outside of the governors if the whole governing body was involved. Broadly, a panel is always the best approach. A reasonable alternative is for a panel to consider a collective grievance and report the facts to the governing body for the governors as a whole to make a decision. The issue of collective grievances needs to be referred to in the revised grievance procedure. In terms of effective handling of grievance, it may be better for the governors to write in the option of consideration by a panel or by the governing body as a whole as options of their choice.

Chapter 5

What is discipline?

Key points

- **Discipline in the employment context**
- **Legal framework**
- **Important differences from grievance handling**
- **Discipline will be a demanding responsibility**

Discipline, in the employment context, is the right of management to set and enforce minimum standards of work and behaviour for staff. These standards must exist if the school is to function effectively. On one level, discipline is a continuous informal process taking place at the workplace on a day-to-day basis. At a certain point, perhaps because of a particular action by a member of staff, the informal maintenance of discipline will not be enough. At this point formal disciplinary action will be taken, through the disciplinary procedure. Such action may ultimately include dismissal.

Legal framework

Balanced against this, there has existed since the mid 1970s a legal right for most employees not be be unfairly dismissed. This means that all disciplinary action takes place within a particular legal framework. For this reason discipline must be fair and consistent, since if it is not it will lead inevitably to a complaint of unfair dismissal being upheld.

Fairness and consistency require a well constructed and well understood disciplinary procedure which is correctly operated.

As with grievance, under LMS governors have a responsibility for overseeing discipline, for setting up the arrangements for discipline, and can expect some direct involvement. The reduction in the role of the Local Education Authority is equally striking and to a degree paradoxical. For example, if the governors decide to make a dismissal the LEA under LMS will do no more than confirm their decision — there is no longer any power vested in the LEA itself to dismiss or otherwise, even in those schools where it remains as the employer and continues to hold the contract of employment. Governors should how-ever consult and take advice from the LEA in dismissal situations.

Important differences from grievance handling

There are some important differences in the ways in which grievance and discipline operate under LMS.

There is an element of urgency about discipline. To be fair discipline must be carried out quickly. If management is contemplating disciplin-ary action, then it must not contemplate it for very long. Any attempt to discipline once too long a time period has passed is bound to be unfair. Worse still is when a member of staff who could and should have been disciplined is not. This does not do the member of staff or the management any good whatever. It can also weaken the position of management if disciplinary action becomes necessary at a later stage. Good staff management means that not only is the disciplinary pro-cedure understood by managers, but that also they do not delay in using it.

Using discipline quickly does not, of course, mean over-using it or attempting to apply disciplinary sanctions which are out of proportion to the disciplinary offence. If, for example, a manager becomes aware of any event which raises the question of possible disciplinary action, it is reasonable to first ask the member of staff concerned for an explanation. To discipline fairly this must be done the same day, not next week or next month.

At the root of discipline is the need by management to set and establish minimum standards. A failure to discipline properly can create a situation where many employees will assume that those standards can be ignored.

An actual example was where members of a staff at a school were borrowing items of school equipment without using the school's established arrangement for booking such equipment in and out. This came to light when the police telephoned the school about one of its video recorders which had been stolen from a member of staff's home. According to school records it was still at the school.

Investigation by the headteacher showed that the abuse of the booking-out system was known to other staff in the school but no corrective action had been taken. There was no question that the member of staff concerned had not taken the video recorder home for school purposes, or that they had not taken reasonable care of it. The member of staff had panicked when it was stolen, and because it had not been booked out did not report its loss to the school. This illustrates how a failure to set and sustain standards created a difficult situation for both the school and the member of staff. Further difficulties could obviously have arisen when the loss of the equipment from the school was detected.

This need for urgency when disciplining also means that any disciplinary procedure has to include the right to suspend. In the case of schools, the ability to suspend a member of staff is, in fact, provided for by the Education Acts. This is the one form of disciplinary action, apart from dismissal, that governors have the right to take directly. In county, controlled and special agreement schools this is also shared with the headteacher. The Articles of Government will establish what the headteacher's position is in an aided school. Secondly, whereas under the grievance procedure it is acceptable to allow the final stage to be the headteacher and for an appeal against the headteachers's decision to be made to the governors, this can not work under the discipline procedure. Here the final stage is dismissal, and it is clear that that decision can only be made by the governors. Furthermore, the governors are required to make arrangements for an appeal against that decision.

This means that the arrangements for discipline, and the disciplinary procedure are more complicated. Added to this, as has already been mentioned, discipline is far more likely to lead to subsequent action through an industrial tribunal if correct procedures are not operated, or discipline is not handled correctly. Although not all staff at a school would necessarily qualify under the law to be able to challenge a decision to dismiss at an industrial tribunal, all staff are entitled to appeal against a decision of the governing body to dismiss.

All of this needs to be taken into account by governors as part of their responsibility for discipline in the school. Any discussion of discipline must refer to dismissal since this is part of discipline. Nevertheless it is only one part of the formal disciplinary procedure and should not allow the purpose of the procedure as a whole to be misunderstood. That purpose is to change the behaviour of the employee, to allow them a further chance before severer penalties are invoked. It is not a punishment nor should it be seen as such.

A further difference between grievance and discipline is that, although discipline takes account primarily of employment behaviour, it is possible for activities outside of employment to become a basis for disciplinary action. An example would be an actual or pending prosecution for a criminal offence. Standards of expected behaviour will of course vary between different organisations. In schools a higher level of personal integrity will obviously be expected because of what schools do. An industrial employer, for example, might tolerate a shop-floor worker being involved with some types of drugs but this would be an entirely different matter for anyone working in a school.

Involvement in formal disciplinary action is a serious matter for any member of staff. Schools operate in a unionised environment and formal disciplinary action will almost certainly mean trade union involvement. This is not to say that the trade union input will be a negative one, but it does mean that procedures and how they are operated will be liable to closer scrutiny than might be the case in other organisations. In schools there is the prospect of disciplinary action arising from the staff/pupil or staff/parent relationship, or both. Clearly any such action will need careful handling.

For any governing body to deal with discipline, requires at least some knowledge of what industrial tribunals have established, over the years, as what is and is not reasonable action by management in the disciplinary field. This will be dealt with in detail later in the book.

As with grievance, there needs to be a clear understanding between the governors and the management of the school as to how discipline will be handled. That the majority of the disciplinary procedure will be handled by the headteacher is not in doubt but certainly suspension, for example, will need special consideration.

Discipline will be a demanding responsibility

The responsibility of governors for discipline will be even more demanding than their responsibility for grievance. It is quite clear that under LMS any decision to dismiss a member of staff can only be made by the governing body, and any appeal against that decision will also be for the governors to determine. Therefore, it is essential that there is an appreciation of what a disciplinary procedure is, what it involves and how it operates. How a school-based disciplinary procedure might work is looked at in detail in the next chapter.

Chapter 6

Disciplinary procedures

Key points

- Why is a procedure needed
- The basic concepts
- The rules of natural justice
- A typical disciplinary procedure
- What else does a disciplinary procedure need to cover

The need for fair and consistent discipline can only be met if there is a properly designed and operated disciplinary procedure. No procedure, however well designed or operated, will mean that every disciplinary decision will be correct; nevertheless, the fact that fair and consistent treatment has been given is both an important contribution to effective staff management and a defence against subsequent action at an industrial tribunal.

Under LMS, the direct involvement of governors in the disciplinary procedure comes at the very end of the process. The end of the disciplinary process means dismissal and clearly the role to be played by the governors is both a vital one and, probably, a difficult one. An appreciation of exactly what the whole of the disciplinary procedure involves is necessary to understand where the governors' role fits in.

The basic concepts of the disciplinary procedure

It may be helpful to look first at the basic concepts. There are two basic concepts behind all disciplinary procedures.

The first concept is that of 'staging'. This is rather like the rungs on a ladder. It means that initially the actual disciplinary steps taken and the level of management involved are the lowest level possible, but increase with each stage of the procedure. The final rung on the ladder is the governing body.

There are several reasons for this staging. In part, it recognises that the disciplinary procedure is attempting to redeem some failing by the member of staff. Clearly both time and opportunity must be given to the member of staff to respond to the disciplinary action. If they do respond, then any further progression up the ladder stops. If they do not, then another rung is climbed.

As with grievance, the approach adopted is still to try and resolve the problem as near as possible to the point at which it started. The first step of the procedure should involve the member of staff and their immediate manager. It falls to that manager to decide whether or not the initial disciplinary action has been successful or whether the next stage should be progressed to.

There will be certain types of disciplinary offence where this gradual progression is simply not appropriate. This is dealt with later in this chapter.

A typical school-based disciplinary procedure

Let us now look at a typical school-based disciplinary procedure as might well operate under LMS. In describing it as typical, it should be said that there are variations in practice. The procedure can be

Diagram 2:   Steps on the disciplinary procedure ladder

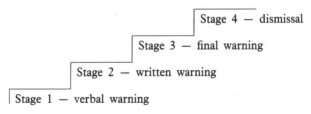

shown diagrammatically as steps on a ladder with the level of seriousness and the level of management involved increasing as each step is
taken.

The different stages of the procedure will be considered first, and
then some other essential aspects which governors need to consider.

Stage 1

'If the immediate manager or supervisor of a member of staff considers
that work behaviour is such as to justify formal disciplinary action, the
situation will be discussed with the member of staff concerned. If
considered justified, a verbal warning may be given. No record of this
verbal warning will be kept on the member of staff's personal record.
The verbal warning will be regarded as lapsed after a period of six
months.'

Not all disciplinary procedures provide for verbal warnings. Their
value is that they can prevent a member of staff from being further
involved in the disciplinary procedure and because no record is kept
they do not add to that person's disciplinary history.

It is also reasonable for a supervisor or equivalent to give a verbal
warning. This bears out the aim of attempting to resolve disciplinary
problems as locally as possible in the first instance. The time limit for
a verbal warning to lapse means that a progression to Stage 2 is only
possible within that time. A further offence after six months would
allow a further verbal warning to be given.

Stage 2

'If within six months of a verbal warning, the immediate manager or
supervisor is not satisfied with the response from the member of staff
concerned he/she may then raise the question of a progression to Stage
2 of the procedure with the head of department or equivalent. The
head of department or equivalent will decide whether Stage 2 should
be initiated. If it is, the member of staff accompanied by a friend or
representative will be requested to attend a disciplinary interview to be
held under Stage 2 of the disciplinary procedure. At least five working
days' notice of the meeting will be given.

'The request to attend the disciplinary interview will include brief
details of the subject of discussion.

'Once the disciplinary interview has been held, the head of department or equivalent will write to the member of staff concerned. The

letter will either state that no further disciplinary action will be taken or will be a written warning.

'As a written warning, the letter will outline the areas of concern to management, what action is required from the member of staff, and give a date at which the situation will be reviewed. The review date will be six months after the disciplinary interview.

'A copy of the written warning, if issued, will be kept on the member of staff's personal file. It will lapse after a period of one year if no further disciplinary action is taken following the review date and will be removed from the file.'

This allows the next level of management to take disciplinary action further. The issue of a written warning is a fairly serious stage of any disciplinary procedure. At the same time, if the member of staff does respond favourably, the written warning will not only lapse but will be removed from file. This gives even an employee who may be in some difficulties in disciplinary terms the opportunity of a fresh start.

Stage 3

'If by the review date specified under Stage 2, no further disciplinary action is considered necessary, a letter to that effect will be sent to the member of staff concerned.

'Alternatively, the head of department or equivalent may raise the question of a progression to Stage 3 of the procedure with the head-teacher. The headteacher will decide whether Stage 3 should be initiated. If it is, the member of staff accompanied by a friend or representative will be requested to attend a disciplinary interview to be held under Stage 3 of the disciplinary procedure. At least five working days' notice of the meeting will be given.

'The request to attend the disciplinary interview will include brief details of the subject of discussion.

'Once the disciplinary interview has been held, the headteacher will write to the member of staff concerned. The letter will either state that no further disciplinary action will be taken or will be a final warning.

'As a final warning, the letter will outline the areas of concern to management, what action is required from the member of staff, and give a date at which the situation will be reviewed. The review date will be six months after the disciplinary interview.

'A copy of the final warning, if issued, will be kept on the member of staff's personal file. It will lapse after a period of two years if no further disciplinary action is taken following the review date and will be removed from the file.'

This stage represents the last within the school management. It allows the member of staff a final opportunity to put matters right before referral to the governors may occur.

Referral to the governors will be for dismissal to be considered.

Stage 4

'If by the review date specified under Stage 3, no further disciplinary action is considered necessary, a letter to that effect will be sent to the member of staff concerned.

'Alternatively, the headteacher will decide whether Stage 4 should be initiated. If the headteacher's decision is that it should be, the headteacher will ensure that the chair of governors and the clerk to the governors are notified. The governing body will convene a disciplinary panel. The disciplinary panel will normally consist of the chair of governors, and two other governors selected by the governing body. The disciplinary panel will be convened within fifteen days of the notification from the headteacher being received. The member of staff will be advised in writing as soon as the date of the disciplinary panel has been arranged and will have the right to attend and to be represented.

'The decision of the panel will be given to the member of staff in writing within 24 hours of the panel reaching its decision. The panel is empowered to take any such decision as it considers appropriate, including dismissal.

'Members of staff shall be dismissed in accordance with the provisions of the Education Act 1988 or equivalent statutory provision.'

This is the final stage of the procedure.

One differencce between grievance and disciplinary procedures is that disciplinary procedures need to make allowance for some particular action by a member of staff which requires a disciplinary response and yet is too serious to be dealt with by applying Stages 1 to 3. Such an action is called gross misconduct and all disciplinary procedures need to make specific provision for it. For example:

Gross misconduct

'Stages 1 to 3 of the disciplinary procedure will not apply where in the opinion of the headteacher of the school the actions of the member of staff concerned amount to gross misconduct. If gross misconduct is alleged, the member of staff will be suspended by the headteacher on full pay, pending further investigation. The headteacher will inform the member of staff in writing of the reasons for and the basis of the suspension. Stage 4 of the disciplinary procedure will then apply except that the suspension shall only be lifted if the disciplinary panel so direct. Subject to the provisions of the Education Act 1988 or alternative legislation, dismissal for gross misconduct will be summary.'

For reasons that will be explained in detail in the next chapter, if gross misconduct is suspected it is essential that the member of staff is suspended, and failure to do so will make subsequent disciplinary action either difficult or impossible. The power to suspend a member of staff is one that governors of many schools can use themselves, however, the advice would be not to use it, in view of the fact that subsequent to suspension they would need to make a disciplinary decision. Gross misconduct implies that the working relationship between the member of staff and the school is destroyed. For this reason if dismissal is upheld then it is immediate subject only to the constraints of education legislation.

A further difference between grievance and disciplinary procedures is that the appeal provisions under a disciplinary procedure need to be more extensive. The important principle with appeals, although it seems obvious, is that no individual dealing with an appeal should in any way have been connected with the original decision. A wording covering appeals might be as follows:

Appeals

1. Stage 2

    'An appeal against a written warning issued under Stage 2 of the procedure should be lodged in writing with the headteacher within 5 days of the written warning being received. The headteacher will invite the member of staff accompanied by a friend or representative to attend an appeal meeting. At least five working days notice of the meeting will be given.

    'Once the appeal meeting has been held, the headteacher will write to the member of staff. The letter will confirm the written warning, withdraw it or substitute a verbal warning under Stage 1.'

2. Stage 3

'An appeal against a final warning issued under Stage 3 of the procedure should be lodged in writing with the chair of governors within 5 days of the final warning being received. The chair of governors will convene a disciplinary appeal panel. The disciplinary panel will normally consist of the chair of governors, and two other governors selected by the governing body. The disciplinary panel will be convened within fifteen days of the appeal being received. The member of staff will be advised in writing as soon as the date of the disciplinary panel has been arranged and will have the right to attend and to be represented. The disciplinary appeal panel is empowered to take any such decision as it considers appropriate, including confirming the final warning, withdrawing it or substituting a written warning under Stage 2.'

3. Stage 4

'An appeal against a dismissal decision under Stage 4 of the procedure should be lodged in writing with the chair of governors within 5 days of the notice of dismissal being received. The chair of governors will convene a disciplinary appeal panel. The disciplinary panel will normally consist of the chair of governors, and two other governors selected by the governing body. The disciplinary panel will be convened within fifteen days of the appeal being received. The member of staff will be advised in writing as soon as the date of the disciplinary panel has been arranged and will have the right to attend and to be represented. The disciplinary appeal panel is empowered to take any such decision as it considers appropriate, including confirming dismissal or substituting a final warning.'

In schools the need for an appeal against Stage 4 (dismissal) is statutory. As such it poses particular problems in the sense that the governors alone make the dismissal decision and it is they who must allow an appeal. As we have seen, governors also would be involved if an appeal is made against a disciplinary decision by the headteacher. It is possible that an appeal to the governors could be made by a member of staff against a final warning, and if that warning is upheld the governors could be involved in making a disciplinary decision under Stage 4.

It is essential that if one member of staff's particular disciplinary situation is dealt with by the governors on more than one occasion that it is put before an entirely different group of governors at each hearing. The chair of governors, for example, having been involved once could not be involved again. This bears out that governors can only deal with discipline by delegating responsibility to small panels. An attempt to put a hearing before the whole governing body would make any further appeal to the governors impossible.

A school disciplinary procedure needs to make provision for a situation where the headteacher might be the subject of disciplinary action. Essentially this would be for gross misconduct. A wording could be included in the section on gross misconduct indicating that if the headteacher is the member of staff concerned then a decision to suspend may be made by the governing body.

It is clear that in most instances governors will be involved in discipline through either disciplinary panels or disciplinary appeal panels. The basis on which these panels should work is a particularly important concept, which underpins the whole disciplinary procedure. That concept is natural justice.

What is natural justice?

This means in practice a set of rules designed to ensure that fair and consistent treatment is given.

The provisions for natural justice do not deal with the merits of a decision but how that decision is made. They are more than a statement of what fair procedure requires. They are a guarantee of the basic rights for both sides. Failure to follow the rules of natural justice is in itself grounds to challenge a decision, however fair it might otherwise be.

For a summary of the rules of natural justice, see Chapter 3.

Disciplinary procedures can lead to dismissal. For this reason appeals must be allowed not only at the final stages but also at the intermediate stages. The appeal provision on first sight may seem excessive, and certainly the implications for governors are considerable. Any school-based disciplinary procedure without reasonable appeal rights does not accord with natural justice. Although governors would be recommended to provide it anyway, this is why the Education Act 1988 requires an appeal right to the governors over a dismisssal decision.

What else does a disciplinary procedure need to cover?

The procedure as outlined above is reasonably detailed. For such a procedure to be workable in practice, there are several issues which need to be addressed.

One is if disciplinary action is being contemplated against trade union representatives. It may be enough to specify that no action will be taken under Stages 1 to 2 without a specific reference to a designated member of management. This would probably be the headteacher.

Secondly, the issue of disciplinary action during probationary service needs to be dealt with. Except on grounds of gross misconduct, where the normal procedure would apply, provision needs to be made for a situation where dismissal is being contemplated during the probationary period. Clearly, the normal disciplinary procedure can not always apply in this situation. Existing industrial tribunal decisions suggest that reasonable steps should be taken to maintain an appraisal of a probationer during their probationary period, giving guidance by advice or warning where necessary. Failure to provide such support could lead to a successful claim of unfair dismissal.

Another issue which should be referred to in the disciplinary procedure is how disciplinary interviews and hearings will be conducted. The guidelines here are the rules of natural justice already detailed, that is to say the right of representation, for both sides to fully present their case, for witnesses to be called and cross-questioned, and for evidence to be presented. A further point is what should happen if information is presented which, in the opinion of the person or panel concerned, requires further investigation. Clearly an adjournment in such an instance is not only necessary but essential, and it is helpful if this is written into the disciplinary procedure.

Finally, reference to the seriousness of grievances arising from discrimination on grounds of disability, race or sex has been referred to in the section on grievance. It is appropriate for the disciplinary procedure to state specifically that discrimination on any of these grounds will be treated as disciplinary offences.

Ultimately, the one major benefit of LMS in terms of effective staff management is that it allows a considerable degree of local flexibility. In the conditions of the 1990s this could be an asset. To make the most of it, governors should ensure that where options are available that the precise circumstances of their particular school are taken into

account. This is especially true where grievance and disciplinary procedures are being revised to operate under LMS. The size and type of
school, and its management structure, will vary from school to school.
So, to a degree, will the grievance and disciplinary procedures. It is
not possible to take one particular grievance or disciplinary procedure
and apply it to a school regardless of the factors mentioned.

Chapter 7

Effective discipline handling

Key points

- **A considerable challenge for governors**
- **Traps for governors**
- **Suspension**
- **Reasonable basis for dismissal**
- **Grounds for dismissal**
- **Implications of disciplinary hearings**

Effective handling of discipline by governors represents a considerable challenge.

That challenge can only be met by a systematic approach to discipline. Firstly this involves a clear understanding of what the disciplinary hearing is for, how it operates and how the governors fit in. This was covered in the last chapter.

The second part of discipline handling for governors is actual involvement, as members of disciplinary or disciplinary appeal panels. As we have already seen, all stages of the procedures up to that level fall to the headteacher and other management staff of the school. It follows that the governors should not expect detailed reports from the headteacher on discipline within the lower levels of the procedure. Nor, in order to preserve their position, should governors be tempted to open up discussion of such cases at governors' meetings.

All governors need to be prepared to be involved in disciplinary hearings. It may be rare for a member of staff to be dismissed, but if it happens there can be no guarantee as to which governors will be available to form the panel. As with grievance hearings, the chair or vice-chair of governors should certainly be designated to chair any meeting of the panel. A clerk is necessary to both set up the meeting and keep a basic record of what happened. This can be the clerk of governors provided that they are not involved in the presentation of the case before the panel in any way.

Although they may opt not to be involved, governors who are also members of staff at the school are not debarred from sitting on disciplinary panels, provided that they are not in any way involved in the disciplinary case. Such governors may well wish to consider carefully whether they would, in practice, wish to be involved. It is possible that the member of staff being disciplined will object to a colleague sitting as a member of the disciplinary panel. Governors faced with such an objection might well be asked to withdraw by the other members of the panel to allow the hearing to proceed.

Again, as with grievance, the most important thing about a disciplinary hearing is that all the parties will be working within the rules of natural justice. Natural justice has been defined in Chapter 3.

It is particularly important that governors who sit on disciplinary panels do not see their role as essentially a passive one, restricted to judging the case on the information presented to them. On the contrary governors should participate fully and should also question and cross-question both sides and any witnesses in order to clarify points.

Doing this requires essentially the same skills as are used during selection interviews. The important key words are 'who', 'what', 'when', 'why' and 'how' — in other words, open questions. Closed or 'yes/no' questions should be avoided. Another important technique is funnelling, a series of open questions followed by a closed one narrowing down on a particular point. For example, 'why did you take it?', 'when did you take it?' followed by, 'wouldn't you agree you were wrong to take it?'

Traps for governors

It is important that governors take notes during the disciplinary hearing and that these notes are kept, since there is the possibility that subsequent referral to an industrial tribunal could occur. These notes should include an outline of questions asked and answers received.

Disciplinary hearings do pose some potential traps for governors. Examples of points to watch for are:

1. Only ask questions that are relevant to the case before you. Avoid leading questions, that is, a question prompting a particular answer. This is more difficult than it seems. For example, if a teacher is being disciplined for allegedly striking a pupil, it would be wrong to ask 'why did you strike the pupil?' It would be right to ask 'what was the pupil doing?', 'what were you doing?', 'what happened next?'

2. Do not allow assumptions, prejudices or stereotypes to influence your decision. The approach should be an evidential one i.e. what decision does the weight of evidence support?

3. You are entitled to assess the credibility of witnesses and the extent to which you accept or reject some or all of their evidence.

4. The value of hearsay evidence can be questionable but it should not be excluded as part of a case.

Suspension

Some of the disciplinary cases that come before the governors will involve instances where members of staff have been suspended. The purpose of suspension needs to be understood. By suspending a member of staff the school is saying that a member of staff's conduct or alleged conduct is such as to destroy the working relationship between them and the school. Suspension is essential where gross misconduct is alleged. Failure to suspend will hamper the subsequent ability to discipline. Let us look at an actual example.

The school caretaker was found smelling strongly of drink in his room at a secondary school. It was clear from his actions that he was not fit to work. The headteacher allowed other school staff to sober him up and the caretaker remained on school premises until the end of the day. A subsequent attempt to dismiss failed because in allowing the caretaker to remain on the premises the headteacher was in practice endorsing that his condition was acceptable.

Similarly, an attempt to suspend two weeks after an event occurred, for which suspension was otherwise appropriate, undermined a subsequent attempt to discipline.

It is relevant for any panel considering a case where a member of staff has been suspended to establish exactly when the event which led to the suspension took place and when the suspension took place.

What the panel needs to do

The most important thing for the disciplinary panel is to correctly identify all the facts of the case. It is then necessary to judge whether what is claimed is correct.

The whole purpose of a disciplinary hearing if it leads to dismissal is to allow the governors to demonstrate that their action has been taken on the grounds of genuine belief, on reasonable grounds and following reasonable investigation. If one or all of these factors is not present, then a decision to dismiss will not only be unfair in law but arguably a wrong decision.

In practice these three factors need to be taken in reverse order.

Reasonable investigation

Governors need to be sure that they do have the full facts before making a decision. The full facts can only be obtained if the panel itself accepts that it has an investigative role. In addition particular instances can arise where the issue of whether or not there has been reasonable investigation is important. It may be helpful to look at an actual example.

A school technician was dismissed following the loss of items of equipment borrowed by other people from the science laboratory in which he worked. On reference to an industrial tribunal it was established that he had never been made aware that his duties included responsibility for ensuring the return of this equipment to the laboratory. This point was not established at the disciplinary hearing.

One particular important element of investigation refers to a situation where a member of staff is being disciplined on the basis of complaints or allegations made by pupils and/or parents. However honest or reliable such witnesses may appear to be, careful investigation is required to substantiate what they say. Without such corroboration it would be unsafe and unwise to proceed on such evidence alone.

Investigation means not only what is the evidence, but also what other information is there to support that evidence.

Another aspect of reasonable investigation is the time factor. In some instances to investigate thoroughly may take time. The important thing here is that the member of staff needs to be informed at the beginning of the investigation that it is proceeding and has some idea of what is being investigated. It is then still reasonable to confront them with the results of the investigation when it is finished, even if this is weeks or months after the investigation starts.

Reasonable grounds

What exactly are reasonable grounds for dismissal?

Since the employment laws which provide the right not to be dismissed unfairly came into existence in the mid-1970s the large number of cases considered by industrial tribunals have built up effectively a series of guidelines as to what will and what will not be unfair dismissal.

The two major grounds for dismissal are capability and conduct. There are other grounds of which absenteeism/sickness is significant for schools. Dismissal on grounds of redundancy is automatically fair dismissal within employment law if the work for which a person was employed has substantially reduced or disappeared. Dismissal on these grounds may be a feature of LMS for the next few years particularly as falling rolls work their way through the secondary sector. Taking industrial action can be a basis for dismissal, this is a drastic step which some industrial employers have taken. The legal implications are complex and detailed and dismissal on such grounds is not likely to involve many, if any, schools.

It is automatically unfair to dismiss a member of staff on the basis of trade union activities or for non-membership of a trade union. This is partly the reason why disciplinary procedures should include some particular provision if disciplinary action is being contemplated against a member of staff who is a trade union representative. Trade union representatives are not, of course, immune to disciplinary action. A representative who, for example, took time off to attend trade union meetings during work-time without using the established arrangements for obtaining time off can be disciplined.

Automatic unfair dismissal for not belonging to a trade union has existed since 1988 and means that if an employee chooses not to join a trade union, or to leave a trade union where a membership agreement or 'closed shop' is or has been in force, they cannot be dismissed. Some

LEAs concluded agreements in the past providing for all staff to be members of the appropriate trade union. Broadly, under LMS, governors would be advised to continue any existing industrial relations arrangements or agreements and it is helpful to know that there is now no basis in law for attempting to enforce membership agreements.

Capability

Dismissal on grounds of capability essentially refers to work performance, the attitude of the member of staff, their ability to sustain good working relationships, and their qualifications.

Work performance is best dealt with by counselling, professional support, and training. Although it may not yet be affecting all schools, the skills-shortage dominated labour market of the 1990s is likely to steer most employers away from disciplinary action on work performance grounds.

Attitude means that difficult or inflexible members of staff can be dismissed on these grounds.

Similarly, an otherwise successful member of staff who can not sustain a good working relationship with other members of staff can be dismissed.

Qualifications refers to qualifications which lapse, or an agreement to acquire a certain qualification as part of taking on the job which is not then acquired. It can be reasonable to dismiss in these situations.

The words 'can be' in all these instances should be noted. In order to dismiss fairly there is a need for the school to show that attempts have been made to support and encourage the member of staff concerned, that supervision has been provided where appropriate, or training if applicable, including time for training to be effective. Only if all such supporting attempts have failed does it become reasonable to dismiss.

A further factor, if dismissal is being contemplated on grounds of capability, is whether alternative employment can be offered. This should be considered. It may be that within a school such alternative employment can be found for some members of staff but mostly, the facility for this is likely to be limited. If alternative employment has been looked at and the school is certain that none is available, it is reasonable to dismiss.

Conduct

Dismissal on grounds of conduct refers primarily to drinking, drugs, absenteeism, dishonesty and criminal activity. Conduct refers primarily to behaviour while at work.

It is possible for any employer to take disciplinary action over certain types of behaviour outside of work. To do this, it must be demonstrated that the behaviour will adversely affect relationships, or damage the relationship between the member of staff and the school.

In the school situation, there may be the possibility of disciplinary action arising from teachers and other members of staff participating in official off-site activities. For example, where negligence by a member of staff leads to injury to a pupil. Disciplinary action is not out of the question but, in practice, such incidents are often such a salutary experience for the member of staff concerned that further action is simply unnecessary. Realistically, such disciplinary action, even if justified, will reduce the willingness of staff to take part in such events.

Drink can be a difficult basis on which to dismiss a member of staff. To merit disciplinary action a serious drink problem is assumed. Most private sector employers offer help rather than discipline. Certainly drink problems may be linked to stress or domestic and personal problems and counselling is a better response. Dismissal will be more difficult if a long-term drinking habit has been tolerated. If attempts have been made to help a member of staff with a drink problem but they have not responded, it may be reasonable to dismiss. Clearly the ability of an organisation such as a school to cope with a person with a drinking problem is bound to be less than some commercial or industrial organisations.

Drugs are a particularly sensitive issue if a school employee is involved. This does not mean that dismissal should be automatic but the particular circumstances do need careful investigation. For example, it would not be fair to dismiss a member of staff convicted on a first offence for possession of cannabis who in court expressed remorse and no support for drug-taking, and whose conduct and work record was otherwise satisfactory. On the other hand, a member of staff convicted for allowing others to grow cannabis in his garden who in court expressed a degree of support for drug-taking could be fairly dismissed.

Dishonesty could include theft of school property but might refer to dishonesty out of school, involving potential criminal activity. Factors to be taken into account include the nature of the alleged offence and the degree of responsibility that the person carries within the school. Certain dishonesty, for example, theft of school property, should be dealt with as gross misconduct.

If a member of staff is being investigated for criminal activities or is going to be prosecuted for criminal activities, special considerations apply. Depending on the offence in question, the issue of gross misconduct arises and it may be appropriate to suspend, pending further investigation.

This is potentially a very difficult area in which to dismiss staff. Broadly, the governors do not have to wait for a police investigation to be completed or for a member of staff to be convicted before dismissing. There must be a reasonable belief that the member of staff is guilty of the offence concerned. For example, if a member of staff has confessed guilt to the police or has been caught red-handed, and this has been established by investigation, it is not necessary to await the outcome of the court case. On the other hand, the fact that a member of staff has been charged with a criminal offence is not in itself reasonable grounds to dismiss. The ability of the governors to investigate a situation may be hampered if police enquiries are pending, for example, a member of staff may refuse to attend a disciplinary panel meeting. If the governors felt they had enough evidence to form a reasonable belief that dismissal was fair, then they could dismiss. In most cases they would be better advised to wait.

If a member of staff receives a criminal conviction, whether it is reasonable to dismiss must depend on the nature of the conviction, and their work record at the school. If a long prison or other custodial sentence is involved then it is clearly fair to dismiss.

Absenteeism/sickness

Absenteeism includes lateness as well as a poor attendance record. Dismissal on these grounds should only be contemplated where absences have been promptly investigated, the member of staff has been given the opportunity to explain, any short-term medical or domestic factors have been taken into account and the member of staff has been warned of the consequences of persistent absenteeism continuing. Even then the age of the member of staff, how long they have worked for the school and the availability of alternative work should all be considered.

Dismissal on grounds of sickness is possible but requires two essential elements. These are that a careful investigation of the medical factors is carried out, and that the member of staff is consulted. The member of staff's own doctor needs to be approached, for which their permission will be required, but consultation with the member of staff means more than that. There must be personal contact between the school and member of staff, discussion of how the sickness is progressing, and consideration of the member of staff's opinion of their own condition. A decision to dismiss must take account of how long the absence due to sickness has been for, and whether alternative employment within the school is possible. It would be appropriate to discuss with the LEA whether the member of staff would be eligible for retirement on ill-health grounds before pursuing dismissal.

Sickness does not extend to pregnant employees. Such employees are entitled to a period of leave before and after the expected confinement, and the right to return to their employment. The issue of dismissal may arise if it becomes impossible for them to carry out their work prior to maternity leave commencing. Dismissal on grounds of pregnancy will automatically be unfair unless the school can demonstrate that no suitable alternative employment exists, and that it has acted reasonably.

Reasonable belief

The disciplinary panel is not required to establish absolute proof but must have reasonable belief that the member of staff is guilty. A disciplinary panel could dismiss a member of staff for dishonesty without a court conviction but this must be based on reasonable belief. For example, there are three witnesses who say they saw a member of staff putting a particular piece of school equipment into the boot of his car and then leaving the school premises. The witnesses appear to be reliable. Investigation shows that the piece of property is missing despite a thorough search of the school. The member of staff concerned denies any responsibility. Police investigations have not established any trace of the property — it is not at the member of staff's home. There is no absolute proof, and a criminal charge either might not be proceeded with or would fail. Dismissal could, however, be made on the grounds of reasonable belief if the governors believe that the member of staff did steal the piece of school equipment.

Reason for dismissal must be stated

To dismiss a person fairly not only requires all the factors already mentioned, but the reason for dismissal must be stated. This is required by law. A reason for dismissal could, for example, be stated simply as on grounds of capability or on grounds of conduct. It seems obvious but the reason given must be the reason why dismissal is taking place. If, for example, both capability and conduct of an employee is used as the basis for disciplinary action it must be stated which is the basis for dismissal or whether it is both. The panel members must be clear on this issue.

Some idea of what could be involved is given in the three disciplinary case studies which appear in Chapter 9.

Implications of disciplinary hearings

Given the extent to which the governing body can be involved in discipline, the question of any report back from a disciplinary panel needs very careful consideration.

Certainly any report back should be delayed until it is clear whether the member of staff intends to use their right of appeal. If there is any discussion by the governing body of a panels' dismissal decision and the member of staff concerned then registers an appeal, that appeal would be impossibly compromised. Similarly, if some governors have been involved in a disciplinary panel and other governors are going to hear an appeal against the panel's decision, then even discussion between governors should be curtailed until the matter has been resolved. It is appreciated that this will be difficult but it is one of the particular implications of school-based disciplinary procedures.

When staff are notified of appeal rights, it is sensible to do so using recorded delivery post and a wording such as ' . . . unless the governors hear to the contrary by (date) it will be assumed that you do not intend to appeal against their decision taken on . . .' . Then, if the right to appeal has not been operated, a report back can be made. There is no particular reason why individual members of staff should be named in such reports.

As with grievance, the purpose of any report to the governing body is to identify whether there are any issues arising which relate to the school's staff management policies, procedures and practices.

Chapter 8

Conclusions and summary

Key points

- **Considerable challenges and risks**
- **A systematic informed approach**
- **The context of grievance and discipline**

It is apparent from the ground covered in the remainder of the book that considerable challenges and risks arise from the change to school-based grievance and disciplinary procedures, which occurs under LMS.

If either the headteacher and management of the school or the governors, or both, do not respond adequately to this situation the effective staff management of the school will be impaired. What is needed, therefore, is a systematic, informed approach. That approach should incorporate some of the elements touched on in detail already:

- An appreciation of the need for well-constructed, revised grievance and disciplinary procedures introduced after consultation with members of staff and trade unions.

- Correct operation of grievance and disciplinary procedures which includes a full understanding and agreement between the management of the school and the governing body on the role each will play in those procedures.

- An appreciation by the governing body that their appeal-panel role in both grievance and discipline must and will hamper the extent to which actual grievances or disciplinary cases can or should be discussed at governors' meetings.

— An understanding of the rules of natural justice and how they apply in either grievance or disciplinary panel situations.

— An awareness that both grievance and disciplinary procedures are essentially problem-solving tools and that failure to use them effectively will hamper the effective staff management of the school.

— An approach to dealing with dismissal cases based on reasonable belief, reasonable grounds and reasonable investigation.

Grievance and discipline do not of course take place in isolation and the reality is that there are many other demands on governors and other essential tasks for them to grapple with under LMS. Nevertheless, poorly handled grievance or discipline cases have the potential to develop considerable additional pressures and problems for schools, out of all proportion to the effort required to handle them correctly in the first place.

Governors can and will be subjected to external pressures when dealing with grievances and staff discipline. These pressures will come from other staff, parents, and trade unions. Some LEAs have allowed trade unions to over-intrude into the disciplinary process in particular. This needs to be firmly resisted at school level. At the same time, although it is apparent that grievance and discipline are school-based under LMS it may not be as apparent that industrial relations become school-based as well. There will need to be a relationship between the governors and the trade unions represented in the school. Setting up LMS-orientated grievance and disciplinary procedures will be an element in that new relationship. Trade union representatives and officials will also be involved in grievance and discipline representing members of staff.

Another demanding context in which governors will be working is the labour market of the 1990s. This is dealt with in more detail in the companion volume on effective staff selection. Essentially shortages of qualified staff can be expected to grow. The private sector of industry and commerce, in particular, is better placed to compete for scarce staff resources than many schools will be. There are some effective options open to schools. In terms of grievance and discipline, the pressure will certainly be to minimise grievance since, as ever, it may translate into increased staff turnover. Similarly, disciplinary action may also be restrained. The pressure will increasingly be to make the best of the members of staff you have and if there are failings to take positive steps to help staff overcome them.

In this situation, it will become even more important that no discrimination on grounds of disability, race or sex occurs. One area where such discrimination can occur is the selection of staff. A job applicant who, for example, is discriminated against on racial grounds could take a case against the governors to an industrial tribunal. They do not need to be a member of staff to do this. This point is dealt with in more detail in the companion volume on effective staff selection.

The point that all governors must be prepared to deal with either grievance or discipline if the need arises, bears repeating. The appeal arrangements if staff are dismissed could involve a considerable proportion of the governing body in the original disciplinary hearing and the subsequent appeal panel. Direct involvement in decisions about whether or not a member of staff should be dismissed can be a disconcerting prospect.

Nevertheless, correct decisions are required and the prospect of involvement can not be accurately forecast. Governors must be prepared to be involved in grievance and discipline, and to appreciate that by being prepared they will be able to make a positive contribution to the effective running of the school.

Chapter 9

Case studies

There are six case studies in all, divided evenly between grievance and discipline situations. The factors that need to be considered under each case study are essentially: What is the problem? Is the member of staff correct or not? Why? Is the headteacher correct or not? Why? What should the governors do about it? Why? A comment on the case studies is given at the end of the chapter.

The case studies illustrate major points already referred to elsewhere in the book and are based on incidents which actually took place. The circumstances described and the names of members of staff are purely fictional, and no resemblance is intended to any actual school or member of staff.

1. Grievance

Case study 1

Bill West, the senior technician, has registered a grievance concerning the conditions in which he has to work at the school. Bill has worked at the school for fifteen years, for ten years as senior technician. Since being promoted to senior technician, he has had an office to himself. The headteacher has just completed a rather hurried reorganisation of accommodation and, as a result, Bill lost his office. He now has to work in a corner of one of the equipment storerooms. The headteacher has said that the best use has to be made of what accommodation is available, and just because Bill is the senior technician, he cannot expect an office all to himself.

Case study 2

Joan Adams, the physical education teacher, moved to this school from another local school at the end of last term. She has registered a grievance because when being interviewed for her present job she claims a series of promises were made which have just not been kept. In particular, she was told that the school gymnasium was about to be totally re-built and re-equipped, and an all-weather athletics track was to be installed. The person she claims made these promises is the previous headteacher who left the school last term. Joan is clearly quite aggrieved and angry, and says she only moved schools because of the promises that were made. She has just discovered that the projects do exist but even a start on them is not expected for some years.

Case study 3

Denise Williams, the headteacher's secretary, has registered a grievance. The headteacher, who has only been at the school for one term, has been concerned that the school switchboard is not manned for a thirty-minute period every lunchtime. Denise has been asked if she would cover the switchboard for this period. She insists that it is not within her job description and seems quite aggrieved. The headteacher agrees that it is not part of her job description but feels that it is not an unreasonable request.

2. Discipline

Case study 4

You are sitting as part of a panel hearing an appeal against dismissal by Owen Richards, the school administrative officer. Owen was dismissed by a disciplinary panel following his conviction for theft of property from a sports club where he works part-time behind the bar.

The chair of governors is chairing the panel. She is looking rather anxiously at her watch. The case has been fully presented except that both sides have not yet had the opportunity to sum up. 'I am getting pressed for time', she says, 'and it would be a waste of my time and yours to adjourn. I propose to give each side ten minutes to sum up so that we will have sufficient time to reach a decision today.' Do you agree?

Case study 5

Brian Smith, one of the assistant school caretakrs, arrived at school one day apparently the worse for drink. He was seen by the headteacher. Brian admitted that he had been drinking heavily the night before and became abusive. The headteacher suspended him and the case is now before you with a recommendation from the headteacher that Brian be dismissed.

The trade union representative is claiming that although drink was a factor, there is a long-term medical condition for which Brian constantly has to take medication and it was the combination of the two that was to blame. The headteacher seems to know nothing of this.

Case study 6

The headteacher recently issued a written warning to Angela Binley, Head of CDT. Angela had taken a number of items of school equipment home without using the booking-out system. 'I only took them home for the benefit of the school,' she says, 'and I always bring them back'. Angela has recently received a verbal warning for the same offence. She seems quite annoyed. 'It's ridiculous that I am being disciplined for this.'

Angela is appealing to a governors' panel requesting that the written notice be withdrawn.

3. Comments on case studies: grievance

Case study 1

Creating a less favourable work environment for a member of staff in this way is likely to damage the relationship between the individual and the school. In view of the hurried nature of the headteacher's action there may have been little or no consultation with staff before changes were made. Bill West has been badly treated and it would not be unreasonable for the governors to instruct that he be given alternative accommodation within the school in keeping with his status as senior technician.

Case study 2

Joan Adams cannot prove that promises were made to her. Arguably she does not need to, since there may be no reason to disbelieve what she says.

Her complaint about the absence of the promised new facilities and equipment may be rooted in inadequacies in the existing facilities and equipment. A commitment could be made to look at that point in conjunction with the headteacher.

Case study 3

What the headteacher has done is not unreasonable. Denise Williams has only been requested to change her duties beyond her job description, there is no question of any unilateral imposition. The grievance should not be upheld.

Discipline

Case study 4

The issue here is natural justice, specifically the right to reply. In the interests of natural justice, that right to reply must be unfettered. An attempt by a disciplinary panel to set time limits would invalidate the entire proceedings.

Case study 5

The point here is whether there has been reasonable investigation. Even if the behaviour of a member of staff is quite unacceptable and drink seems to be the sole factor, investigation is required to establish whether there are any other contributory factors. In this case there apparently was and investigation will be needed before the panel can reach a decision.

Case study 6

The panel would be correct in upholding the headteacher's action. This is an example of where the disciplinary procedure is being correctly used to enforce reasonable managerial standards. The implications of Angela Binley continuing to breach the rules regarding school equipment are apparent and it is not in her interests or the school's that she continues to do so.